NEW YORK/NEW YORK

JOHN HALPERN was born in New York City in 1918 and attended Dartmouth College. He has been a television director at two major advertising agencies. During that time he met Margaret Bourke-White, and she encouraged him to become a photographer. He received further encouragement from Edward Steichen and Berenice Abbott. Mr. Halpern then worked on documentary films for the Massachusetts Institute of Technology and Time-Life, Inc., which were shown on television and in classrooms. Since he had always been interested in architecture, he proposed and has been working on an ongoing project for the Avery Library of Columbia University called "The Changing Face of America," which documents architecture photographically, both past and present, from New England, the Middle Atlantic States, and California.

John Halpern

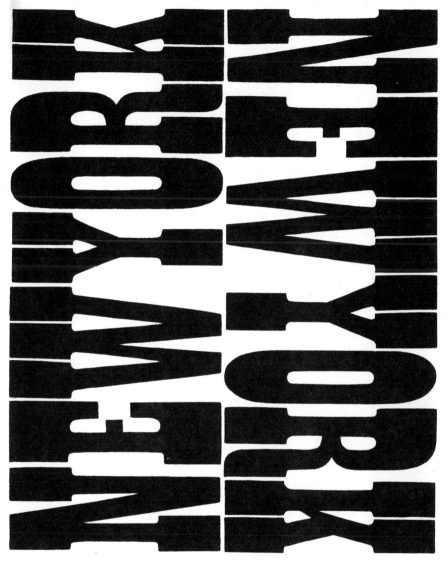

AN ARCHITECTURAL PORTFOLIO

A DUTTON PAPERBACK | E. P. DUTTON | NEW YORK

To my wife, my children,
the friends who have given
much valued encouragement,
and Eugène Atget.

CONTENTS

Color insert follows page 22.

..WALT WHITMAN..

Ah, what can ever be more stately and admirable to me than mast-hemm'd Manhattan?

"Crossing Brooklyn Bridge"

Superb-faced Manhattan!

"A Broadway Pageant"

Manhattan's streets I saunter'd pondering
On Time, Space, Reality—

"Prudence"

NEW YORK / NEW YORK
An Architectural Overview

Mrs. Trollope might well have had James Hardie in mind when she observed that Americans had an egregious proclivity for bombast. One might take the more charitable view that he was merely giving expression to another native trait—ingenuous enthusiasm—when he stated, in 1827, "The extensive patronage extended to the liberal arts and works of taste, the unexampled increase of public amusements, with the consequent progress of morals and refinement, have at length rendered New York the Paris of America." [1]

In truth, New York at that time had the look of a prosperous middling-size, provincial English town, which, from an aesthetic point of view, was very nice indeed. It was a city of red brick buildings whose walls were accented with sparkling white window trim and Adamesque doors. New York seemed as Georgian as Dublin.

The physical resemblance to Dublin was further emphasized by its commercial buildings. The few that remain today on South Street and Fulton Street still have their counterparts in Ireland and England.

A sense of Englishness was quite natural. In the early part of the nineteenth century the residents of New York were mostly of English descent. Although political independence had been achieved, culturally, the country, especially in its larger cities, was still a colony.

After the Revolution, another style of architecture began to appear, a form of modified Georgian that was somewhat chauvinistically labeled Federal. If Georgian can be considered toned-down Baroque, Federal is toned-down Georgian, resembling it but simpler in its decorative accouterments and more austere in its lines. Symbolic of the chauvinism is the gold American eagle standing atop the entranceway, lintel wings outspread as if on the ready.

In New York there are still many Federal residences—entire blocks of them—that are occupied and in fine condition, to be found mainly in the Greenwich Village area of Manhattan, but also in the Cobble Hill and Brooklyn Heights sections of Brooklyn.

Lord Byron accomplished a good deal more than he probably realized when he gave time, effort, and money to the cause of Greek liberation from

---

[1] James Hardie, *The Description of the City of New York,* 1827.

1

1. 2 White Street. c. 1780. Possibly the oldest building in the city.

2. 56 Middagh Street. 1829. Late Federal style.

the Turks. We had our revolution, the French theirs, and now it was the Greeks' turn, with the assistance of a brave, handsome, and aristocratic English poet. Could the stage for the age of Romanticism have been better set?

Revolution was in the air on the Continent and rapid evolution was taking place in England. What better than to see in the ancient Greeks those ideals that might well be applied to the present? A romantic thought that was to find outlets in all the arts, including architecture.

Accordingly, around 1830, public institutions, churches, and large houses took on a Greek look. Massive pediments and Doric columns were the order of the day.

If architecture is accepted as reflecting a state of mind, what Americans at the time were thinking is quite obvious. They were the new Greeks.

Accepting certain premises, they had a point. Ancient Athens *was* a democracy, and although the United States was constituted a republic, the citizenry tended to regard themselves as free and equal democrats. Equally important was a desire to free this country from English cultural domination.

Unlike the descendants of the pre-Columbians in Latin America, North Americans had no native architectural heritage upon which to build. A tepee is hardly a match for an Aztec temple. In lieu, therefore, of an indigenous tradition to fall back on, classic Greek architecture was revived as the best available expression of the way in which America regarded itself—simple, yet majestic, dignified, and beautiful.

A city such as New York was ideal for this architectural *nouvelle vague.* The population, around 200,000 at the time, was growing in leaps and bounds and had need for larger buildings to house its commerce, religious congregations, and government offices.

Although nearly all of the original Greek Revival buildings that were done in the grand manner for government and commerce have disappeared, a number of churches in this style remain. Also extant is the former Sub-Treasury building at Wall and Nassau streets, looking for all the world like an authentic Greek temple seated incongruously among the mass of skyscrapers that tower above it.

As has happened so many times before in history, a disaster provided the opportunity for new approaches and improvements. The great fire of 1835 practically destroyed the commercial center of the city, leveling everything in its path from Broad to Wall to South streets.

Within two years, 1836–1837, the business community presented the new look of Greek Revival for the world to admire. And there was much to admire. The red brick and white trim of the Georgian and Federal styles was preserved, but the buildings were larger than their predecessors, usually four or five stories in height. Their essential "Greekness" was generally confined to the ground-floor front, and this was almost pre-classic in its austerity and simplicity—plain pilasters and flat lintels.

3. St. John's in the Village, 224 Waverly Place. 1846. The "stone" columns are made of stucco on wood.

There were by this time enough New Yorkers who were able to consider themselves rich enough to afford mansions, if not palazzi. Affluence equal to the requirements necessary for entry into that league had to wait a few decades. Fortunately, the current flair for Greek Revival suited both their aspirations and their pocketbooks. Unfortunately, no large houses of that period remain.

Still extant, however, are Greek Revival row houses, the handsomest examples being those situated on the northern end of Washington Square. Henry James, a former resident, would have no trouble recognizing them today, as they are in mint condition. Currently, they house the offices and fraternities of New York University, and the types who formerly would have occupied them consider themselves lucky to be living in the reconverted carriage houses directly behind the row.

The *AIA Guide to New York City* describes New York's iron-front buildings as ". . . one of the most glorious commercial groupings that New York had ever seen . . ." The only carping here is with the words *one of the.* There are those who would insist on *the.*

Grigori Potemkin, who put a pretty front on a good part of Russia in order to please Empress Catherine II, would have been delighted with the concept underlying these improbably lovely buildings, namely to cloak mundanity with a mantle of beauty. What would have been ordinary lofts emerge as Renaissance Palladian palazzi, uniquely interesting.

Their specialness lies in the fact that, unlike the tradition they emulate, they present vast expanses of glass decoratively framed, giving them, no matter how large, a quality of grace and airiness. And the wonder of it is that it is all a facade, a remarkable synergism of technology and creativity.

If one man is to be credited with this rapid efflorescence of cast-iron prefabrication it is James Bogardus (1800–1874). In the early 1840s he traveled throughout Italy, was enthralled with the architecture he saw, and decided to adapt it to cast-iron prefabrication.

His place of business, The Eccentric Mill Works, at Centre and Duane streets, was built entirely of prefabricated parts and was assembled in two months. Contemporary drawings reveal it to be quite unlike any building of its time; it is, indeed, most forward-looking in its appearance. It was the only building of its kind that he ever had the opportunity to construct. Possibly, the existing establishment of bricklayers, hod carriers, carpenters, and stonemasons looked not too kindly upon the prospect of buildings that could be put together with a spanner wrench.

Only one work by James Bogardus remains, his own warehouse at 85 Leonard Street. There was, until a few years ago, another, the Laing Building, which stood alone and bedraggled on the corner of Washington and Murray streets. Built in 1848, one of his first creations, it was a veritable

4. 72–76 Greene Street. 1876. J. F. Duckworth. The king of Greene Street, happy hunting ground for iron-front enthusiasts.

gem. The building was torn down in 1971, and the facade was piled in an adjoining vacant lot. The unguarded pile was later stolen by thieves for scrap metal, which speaks volumes on the subject of current priorities.

There were other architects—Samuel A. Warner, Henry Fernbach, Griffith Thomas—who made their mark in the field of cast-iron architecture, but Bogardus stands out as the great originator.

The era of cast iron waxed throughout the period 1850–1870 and then waned suddenly after a series of disastrous fires proved that not only was cast iron not fireproof, as had been previously thought, but was also a fire hazard due to its propensity for melting and buckling.

Before that fiery moment of truth, the cast-iron prefabrication industry flourished mightily in New York, not merely confining itself to the city, but classing up facades ranging from Nova Scotia to Egypt. In this country many a small-town office building, somewhere on its handsome cast-iron front, bore the legend "Made in New York."

Cast-iron ornamentation of all shapes and sizes—filigree work, statues, fountains, balustrades, cigar-store Indians—blossomed all over the place, including much of that famous New Orleans filigree. Like the buildings, they had their day, but while it lasted, it was exuberant.

"That man is a brownstone!"

In the 1850s any individual so called was recognized as a person of substance and respectability. He and thousands like him could afford the luxury of homeownership, provided it did not entail too much of a dip into his pocketbook. This of course necessitated compromise: "Mr. Would-Be-Homeowner, you can have a house within your means, but you must settle for uniformity."

We all know what mass production means, and most of us credit the concept to Henry Ford. In reality, the credit should go to those speculator-builders who managed to color New York brown in a matter of decades. Although the bulldozer had not been conceived even in nightmares, the zeal with which hands and horses tore down the old and leveled the greenery was unprecedented.

The new breed of builder employed mass methods almost worthy of a William Levitt. No longer a carpenter-builder himself, he was a contractor, having at his disposal all manner of building specialists—joiners, lathers, plumbers, and bricklayers.

Even as the brownstone row houses were rising, they were dismissed by contemporary critics as a jerry-built, maudlin mass of dullness. Later, sociologists observed that the brownstone era did more to change the physical and psychic character of New York than anything that had previously taken place.

That there was a critical need for housing was a point upon which everyone agreed. The population of the city and its environs had almost doubled within the decade 1840–1850, achieving the substantial total of 696,115 by the latter date. The housing shortage was chronic then, as it would continue to be up to the present day, and the brownstones, row upon row, seemed an excellent solution.

The logic of the row houses was eminently well suited to the city's grid plan and standardized lot dimensions, a narrow rectangle twenty feet wide and one hundred feet in depth. A whopping number of houses could be jammed together on one city block. The uniform brownstone fronts were no more than a comparatively thin veneer covering brick and wood.

Brownstone interiors were all alike. Everything was long and narrow—

5. 72 Willow Street. c. 1850. Early brownstone.

the stoops, the windows, the front and back rooms. Housekeeping could be something of a chore in that it involved a good bit of stair climbing—four flights from cellar to top story—but maids were cheap and plentiful. Who can ever forget the scene in *Life with Father,* when Clarence Day walks into an employment agency for immigrant Irish girls, looks around the room, makes a quick choice, and roars, "I'll take that one!" Spoken like a true brownstone!

The "Brown Pall," [2] as Lewis Mumford put it, extended all over the city, and then the quarries gave out. Row houses were still rising but without the brownstone face. Red or yellow brick had to make do, but not for long.

More than an era was over; a way of life had reached its end. The one-family house for the middle class had become luxury beyond its reach; land was becoming far too valuable for single housing.

The brownstones themselves? Hundreds still stand, many in fine shape, many shabby and sad looking. Because brownstone is a rather soft type of sandstone, time and weather have treated it most unkindly, and these depredations have given many brownstones the appearance of a used cake of brown soap.

Contemporary students of the Victorian period seem to concur in regarding that era as a time when society—in England and America—was dominated by personalities who were steady, sober, and strong on the outside, all the while seething on the inside. One recalls a later prototype, the minister-rapist of Somerset Maugham's "Rain."

Less esoteric, but equally germane to any explanation of the Victorian aesthetic, is the relationship of the Industrial Revolution to life at the time and the manner in which technology and its progenitors influenced the arts.

A new breed of individual attained the wealth, power, and social recognition previously restricted to a single, tightly knit class, the landed aristocracy. This "new man," the manufacturer, was not a knowing patron of the arts or an individual to hedonism born. He was the Lord Murphy of Tennessee Williams's *Camino Real,* whose patent of instant nobility was obtained through large contributions to the party in power. His American counterpart received the accolade, of nobility, figuratively—"merchant prince," "robber baron," "mining king," etc.

The type, both here and in England, had a desire to express its exaltedness in the time-honored manner: great houses. They wanted their homes to flaunt what manner of men they were; and if architects and builders are to be judged solely on the basis of giving the customer what he wants, then the Victorian gentlemen of these callings may be said to have done themselves proud. Although many of their creations were os-

[2] Lewis Mumford, *The Brown Decades, a Study of the Arts in America, 1865–1895* (New York: Dover, 1955.)

6. 294 West 71st Street. c. 1885. Romanesque window and classical doorway, true
Victorian Eclectic.

tentatious, vulgar, heavy-handed, and forbidding, they expressed the Victorian *Geist* more eloquently than any other art form.

Montgomery Schuyler had this to say of a later Victorian style, an observation that can really be applied to the entire spectrum: "Queen Anne is a comprehensive name which has been made to cover a multitude of incongruities, including, indeed, the bulk of recent work which otherwise defies classification, and there is a convenient vagueness about the term which fits it for that use." [3]

The key words in attempting to define architecture during Victoria's reign are *revival* and *eclectic*. New York's famous prison, the original Tombs at 100 Centre Street was described as "Egyptian Revival," because it looked vaguely Egyptian. A good example of eclectic would be the quite remarkable Jefferson Market Court House at 425 Avenue of the Americas. Just how eclectic may be deduced from the fact that so erudite an observer as Alan Burnham has said, "It may best be described as Victorian Gothic." [4]

"Work which otherwise defies classification" is the stuff of Victorian eclecticism. On more than one occasion will a scholar of the genre label a given structure "Germanic Renaissance/Eclectic" while an equally learned colleague will insist that it is "French Renaissance/Eclectic."

A look through the charming pictures in John Betjeman's *Victorian and Edwardian London: From Old Photographs* [5] illustrates the point once again: what was stylish in London set the style for New York. Tottenham Court Road, Oxford Street, and Regent Street (c. 1875) looked for all the world like sections of lower Broadway, Union Square, and upper Greenwich Street.

By 1890, the Colonial-Federal-Greek-Revival look had all but disappeared in New York. The city now incorporated all five boroughs, and its residents occupied the approximate areas they are living and working in today. The world looked on in wonder at the manner in which the city tore itself down and built itself up again. The new look was essentially Victorian. The Upper West Side, the East Side, Harlem, and Brooklyn are veritable treasure troves of Victoriana.

When, in the early part of this century, Andrew Carnegie was presented with a federal income tax bill of over $500,000, which represented ten percent of his total earnings for that year, he was sure the country was going to the dogs. This, however, did not prevent him from erecting a

---

3 Montgomery Schuyler, *American Architecture: Concerning the Queen Anne* (New York: Harper & Brothers, 1892).

4 Alan Burnham, ed., *New York Landmarks* (Middletown, Conn.: Wesleyan University Press, 1963).

5 New York: The Viking Press, 1969.

7. 1 Sutton Place. Remodeled 1921. Once the home of Mrs. William K. Vanderbilt, it is now the official residence of the Secretary General of the United Nations.

palace, costing roughly his year's gross income, on an entire blockfront of Fifth Avenue.

He was not alone. *Le Bourgeois Gentilhomme*, American style, was richer than the wildest imaginings of Molière's original, and, like him, now had access to professional taste makers. Also, like him, he meekly followed instructions in the niceties, which for architecture was the "French look."

Names of importance appeared in the architectural firmament—Richard Morris Hunt, D. H. Burnham, and the prestigious firms of McKim, Mead and White, and Carrère and Hastings. Owning an edifice designed by any of these gentlemen was a supreme status symbol. They took the Paris of Baron Haussmann as their model, quite understandably, since most of them received their architectural education at the Ecole des Beaux-Arts, whose tenets gave Paris the eclectically classical look so characteristic of that beautiful city.

The result of the new trend was a spate of mansion building unprecedented in history. Upper Fifth Avenue, the side streets between Fifth and Park avenues, Riverside Drive, and West End Avenue effloresced with a visual approximation of Paris. In general it may be said that the large town houses on the West Side were somewhat more fanciful and flamboyant and, oddly, gave more of a feeling of the Continent than their neighbors across the park.

It was second- and third-generation wealth whose houses reflected the more restrained taste of a bygone era. Once again Georgian and Federal appeared, with an occasional touch of Ivy League Gothic rounding out the scene. The age of mansion building declined rapidly just prior to World War I and came to a virtual standstill during the Depression.

There are still numerous owner-occupied town houses, most of them on the side streets of the Upper East Side. And in the grand tradition of old, there are blocks of beautiful private dwellings facing Gramercy Park, on Beekman Place, and Sutton Place. As yet, in these locations, there is no inkling whatsoever of 1984.

Commerce and crowding once again made involuntary changes in lifestyle a must for many people. If they chose to stay in Manhattan, they had to move into what was considered by some people to be nothing more than high-class tenements, newfangled put-ons called "French flats," a euphemism for apartment houses.

To the cliff dweller of today, who pays for the privilege of living in a low-ceilinged affair whose thin walls make his neighbor's more intimate habits —sonically at least—as familiar to him as his own, the plight of those "unfortunates" who gave up their private houses in order to endure the Dakota or the Osborne would only fill him with murderous envy. The tenants of such buildings had to make do with forty-foot living rooms, ceilings reaching fifteen feet, walls whose thickness would do justice to a

8. San Remo Apartments, 145 Central Park West. 1930. Emery Roth. Art Deco was on the rise, but Mr. Roth chose the fancy opulence of the 1920s.

fort, heavy, mirrored doors with brass trimmings that are collector's items today, and solid marble fireplaces.

The first of these, standing alone in all its Germanic glory when it was first built in 1884, was the Dakota of Henry Hardenburgh, who also conceived the equally opulent Plaza Hotel. Old photographs of this great apartment house show it situated on West 72nd Street in the middle of a vast open space. To its first occupants it seemed as if they were as far from the center of the city as those living in the Dakota Territory, thus the reason for the delightful name.

Many other equally luxurious apartments afforded a new sense of grandeur to the concept of collective residential construction. Between the 1880s and 1910 they appeared in locations as far apart as lower Fifth Avenue and Lenox Avenue in Harlem. A number of them occupied an entire city block, ensuring ample light and air in addition to a felicitous view because of large, attractively landscaped center courtyards.

The great surge of apartment-house construction was by no means confined to superluxe facilities. Middle-income apartments appeared in overwhelming numbers throughout the Upper West Side, in Harlem, and on Lexington and Madison avenues on the Upper East Side. Their exteriors were, in many instances, even more ornate than their more glamorous counterparts on Riverside Drive and Central Park South.

If in the early 1900s one had gazed upon the seemingly endless panorama of mansions lining upper Fifth Avenue, "It can't happen here" would have been the rejoinder to any thought he may have entertained regarding the possibility of their falling victim to the wrecker's ball within the space of a couple of decades. Nevertheless, those four apocalyptic horsemen—inflation, depression, taxes, and servant shortage—accomplished just that.

Most of the mansions were reduced to rubble prior to the outbreak of World War I, but the apartments that replaced them need not be the cause for shedding tears on behalf of their occupants, unless twenty- to thirty-room "digs," many with vast expanses of terrace and fantastic views, can be considered "making do."

When upper Fourth Avenue became Park Avenue as a result of the Grand Central Terminal's tracks being covered over to make a boulevard in the early part of the century, *Park Avenue Swell* was soon added to the lexicon to describe those who lead the affluent life.

The first apartments appeared near the area of the terminal, and they represented a new triumph in the annals of engineering since they were supported on shock-proof foundations extending down through the street surface to the railroad yards below. Rumble and vibration from passing trains were reduced to a minimum. Here was an urban-renewal project on the grand scale indeed. Fifty blocks extending from 46th Street to 96th Street were transformed from a run-down area resembling the rail approaches to Glasgow to one of the most fashionable residential streets in the world, which it still remains.

Since World War II, scads of gargantuan apartment buildings, whose general architectural style might be described as "Contemporary Undistinguished," have been erected.

Philip Birnbaum, an architect who has designed almost two hundred apartment houses throughout the city, explained with exemplary frankness in The New York Times in 1970 the philosophy underlying the construction of these new buildings: "The builder is not a philanthropist. . . . To increase his rent roll, he must get more apartments in the same amount of space and fill up the building in a hurry." Small wonder that apartments in older buildings many times command higher prices! Commercial necessity was the driving force behind the erection of New York's first skyscraper.

A young silk merchant, John Stearns, bought a lot at 50 Broadway in the spring of 1887, and to pun a bit, he paid a lot for that lot. Good businessman that he was, he figured, quite logically, that if he could rent office space additional to his own needs, he would not only recoup his original expense, but would ensure himself a handsome profit through the years. The obstacle to this line of reasoning was the width of the lot, twenty-one and a half feet. The decision that he made to overcome this obstacle was to affect the future of New York beyond anyone's imagining; he decided to maximize the space.

With that purpose in mind, he engaged the services of a young New York architect, Bradford Lee Gilbert. It was Mr. Gilbert who envisioned steel-cage construction as the ideal method for meeting Mr. Stearns's requirements. His plan more or less resembled that of an upended bridge supporting thin covering walls. The cage would support the walls, a revolutionary concept. That the architect had confidence in the safety of the structure (apparently he was one of the few who did) was evidenced when he announced that he planned to locate his offices on the top floor.

Proof of Gilbert's faith in his creation came in the form of a hurricane. The building was near completion in 1889, when hurricane-force winds buffeted the city on a Sunday morning. Both Gilbert and Stearns rushed from their homes to the site where they found crowds awaiting the building to topple. The men clambered their way to the top, and in the middle of the howling gale, Gilbert dropped a plumb line from a front corner to the street below. He announced with pride that there was not the slightest indication of vibration. Because it "towered into the sky," John Stearns named his thirteen-story "skyscraper" the "Tower Building."

The great skyscraper race was on, and America's cities were never to be the same. By 1913, when the sixty-two-story Woolworth Building at 233 Broadway was completed, the streets of Lower Manhattan had become the now-familiar canyons of steel and stone.

The early skyscrapers were as much a triumph of engineering as of architecture. With the advent of this revolutionary method of construction, and its apparently limitless possibilities of scale, there was no architectural

9. Metropolitan Life Insurance Company Building, 1 Madison Avenue. 1909. Napoleon Le Brun & Sons. Lloyd Morgan's remodeling in 1962 emphasizes the Directoire grandioseness of the campanile.

precedent as a point of reference, so decorative devices of the past were employed as a thin veneer to cover the steel towers soaring toward the sky.

How does one make an architecturally interesting statement from a basically monolithic shaft rising, perhaps, to a height of forty stories or more above street level? The answer lay in the field of view covered by the human eye. Most people in going about their day-to-day affairs look neither up nor down very much. They do look straight ahead and from side to side on occasion, glancing upward now and then to relieve the monotony.

This must have been the logic that dictated early skyscraper architecture. How else does one explain the accepted procedure of decorating the devil out of the bottom and the top and more or less letting the middle fend for itself? The first skyscrapers were not so tall that their entire facades could not be bedizened with all sorts of gimcrackery. It was their somewhat later neighbors that sported fancy tops and bottoms. In lieu of a helicopter, the 500mm telephoto lens opens up a vista rarely beheld by the human eye—close views of the older skyscraper roofs. Some of them resemble mad King Ludwig of Bavaria's looniest fantasies come true; others, the temples at Angkor Wat in Cambodia.

Perhaps the circle is coming full turn as a contemporary architect, Ulrich Franzen, describes his design for a thirty-three-story apartment building at 800 Fifth Avenue as having a "stern proper bottom breaking into a joie-de-vivre top."

The Chrysler Building, a new kind of skyscraper, dominated the New York skyline when it was completed in 1929—a perfect expression of Art Deco. It was very different—an immense expanse of white brick ornamented with stainless steel gargoyles resembling gigantic radiator caps and with abstract designs similair to hubcaps.

Art Deco was an import from France. Its use here occasionally caused some rather bizarre transmutations in the attempts of our native designers and architects to create American versions, but they effectively fitted the need to break away from the classical restrictions of the past in the continuing development of the skyscraper, which was a unique American contribution to world architecture.

The current fashion of latter-day Bauhaus is in vogue, not only in New York but all over the world, because it nicely meets the requirements of maximum return on minimum investment. There are drawings in The Museum of Modern Art done by Ludwig Mies van der Rohe in 1919 of steel-and-glass office buildings that could take their place on Park or Fifth avenues today were they to be realized, and they would look just about as contemporary as anything on those streets.

To the world at large, New York City is the borough of Manhattan. It is this small island, thirteen and a half miles long and two and a fourth miles wide, whose towering buildings, glistening in the sun by day and glittering with millions of lights by night, give it an appearance unique unto itself.

Edith Wharton long ago in *A Backward Glance* made the darkly foreboding prediction that New York would become a chapter in prehistory, "as much a vanished city as Atlantis or the lowest layer of Schliemann's Troy." [6]

Le Corbusier was somewhat more sanguine in his estimation that New York is "A city that will be replaced by another city." He also said, "The skyscrapers are too small." Even the mind of Baron Haussmann, who created the great squares in Paris, would have boggled at his compatriot's solution to the problem.

Le Corbusier proposed razing the entire city and then building a string of ten or more 300-story Goliaths running the length of Manhattan down its center, with the remaining land to be landscaped into a vast and beautiful park.

This, obviously, has not occurred, but his criticism concerning size, at least, has been rectified: the skyscrapers have become *much* bigger.

And Miss Wharton's gloomy view has a certain validity. The older skyscrapers, whose outline filled Le Corbusier with such awe and enthusiasm, have been all but obliterated from view, buried beneath the gigantism of their newer, shining steel, glass, and concrete neighbors. This has caused the fear eloquently expressed by Alan Burnham: "When all our buildings have become glass cubes, drama will be lost to unending dreariness. The picturesque skyline of the latter part of the nineteenth century and the early twentieth is vanishing. . . ." [7]

Interestingly, critics in the 1850s were similarly fearful that "unending dreariness" would be the city's fate as a result of the brownstone craze and that every last vestige of the rich Federal and Greek Revival heritage would become mere memory.

These dire predictions have not yet come to pass, and an increasing awareness, both on the part of the public and officialdom, that an architectural heritage is not something to be dismissed lightly may ensure that they never will.

There are literally hundreds of buildings throughout the city representing, with the exception of Early Colonial, every architectural style developed in each epoch of the city's history. Unlike Williamsburg, they are not reconstructed museum pieces but places where people live, work, and worship, just as they have been doing from the early part of the nineteenth century right up to the present.

True, the activities within any given building probably have changed

---

6 Edith Wharton, *A Backward Glance* (New York: D. Appleton-Century Co., 1934).

7 Burnham, ed., *op. cit.*

10. 759 Second Avenue. c. 1905. "A city which will be replaced by another city."—
Le Corbusier

over the years. Buildings that were commercial lofts—some well over a hundred years old—in the area south of Houston Street called SoHo are now humming with the creative activity of the artists who are their new residents. Small spaces that were once "Mom and Pop" candy stores have been transformed into fascinating boutiques, and old tenements are the locations for colorful bars and cafés. Many of these places are situated in areas where they are surrounded by some of the most contemporary architecture in the world.

One of the major attractions of any great city is walking around and "seeing the sights." The same holds true, of course, for a New England village or a Colorado mining town, but a city does have one advantage— immense variety. In New York it is all there for the seeing and the savoring —the old and the new, the large and the small, the mundane and the magnificent.

The following photographs do not pretend to be a complete visual record of every architectural point of interest that New York has to offer; that would require volumes. They do, however, cover the architectural styles and a number of the charming "mundanities" that have been a source of delight to at least one individual, the photographer/author.

1. 62 Pearl Street. 1827. A classic of its kind, still humming with activity.

2. James Watson House, 7 State Street. 1793–1806. Attributed to John McComb, Jr. The only survivor of the first mansions, it is now the shrine of Saint Elizabeth Seton.

3. 96 Greenwich Street. c. 1828. Once a residence, it is now the "Pussycat Lounge."

4. View from the World Trade Center toward Reade Street. A lot of old-timers down there are lucky to have escaped the mass razing of the nearby Washington Market.

5. St. Paul's Chapel, Broadway and Fulton Street. 1766. Thomas McBean. George Washington *may* have slept here during the sermon, but it is a fact that he worshiped here. St. Paul's is the only pre-Revolutionary building still standing in the city.

6. Department of Health, Hospitals and Sanitation, 125 Worth Street. 1933. Charles P. Meyers. Beautifully oxidized bronze Art Deco sculpture.

7 (*left*). Potter Building, 38 Park Row. 1883. N. Y. Starkweather. This magnificent Victorian office building boasts the first pressed terra-cotta facade in New York. 8 (*above*). 11 Willow Street, Brooklyn Heights. c. 1875. Obviously old, but in terms of the "Heights," a Victorian newcomer.

9. 24 Middagh Street, Brooklyn Heights. 1824. The former Eugene Boisselet House, generally considered to be the top attraction in Brooklyn Heights.

10. Manhattan Bridge. 1905. Gustav Lindenthal, engineer. Not nearly so famous as its neighbor to the south—the Brooklyn Bridge—it is nonetheless regarded as one of the world's great bridges.

11. 74–76 Greene Street. 1876. J. F. Duckworth. One of the main stops on lecture tours in the "cast-iron district."

12. 135 East Houston Street. c. 1870. The mansard roof of this derelict little gem adds to its poignance.

13. 328 Bleecker Street. c. 1880. It could well be a backdrop for *The Saint of Bleecker Street*.

14. 127–131 MacDougal Street. 1829. Built for Aaron Burr, these village landmarks are next-door neighbors of the famed Provincetown Playhouse.

15. 512–518 Hudson Street. 1840. Like all old beauties, this one looks even better "all dolled up."

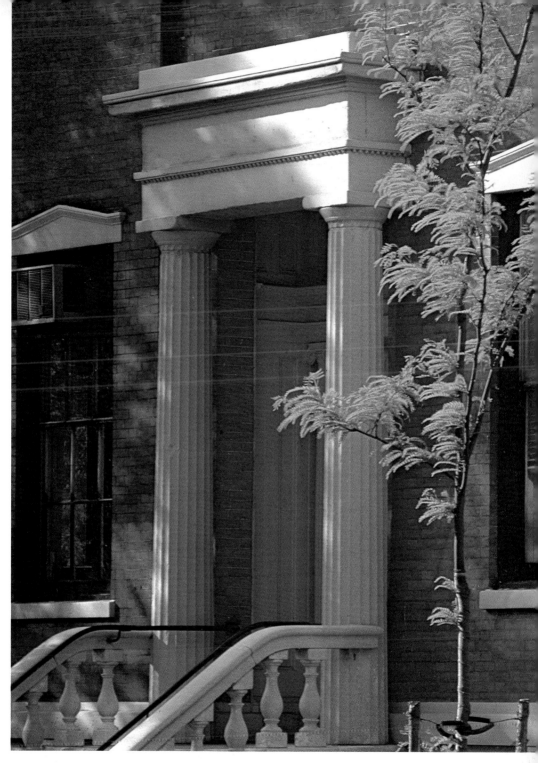

16. 4 Washington Square North. 1833. One can almost imagine Edith Wharton and her friend Henry James walking out the door—and with reason—they both were residents of "the Row."

17 (*above*). 134–136 First Avenue. c. 1890. Fancy pressed-steel roof or no, this is still a tenement. 18. (*left*). Flat-iron Building, 949 Broadway. 1902. D. H. Burnham & Co. The north end of the great building that, for a short while, was the tallest in the city.

19 (*right*).Chrysler Building, 405 Lexington Avenue. 1930. William Van Alen. What with gigantic radiator caps for gargoyles and its incredible stainless-steel roof, this marvelous Buck Rogersish edifice is the ultimate homage to the automobile. It was completed just in time for the Great Depression.

20 (*above*). New York Yacht Club, 37 West 44th Street. 1899. Warren & Wetmore. A most fanciful Beaux-Arts representation of a mighty eighteenth-century frigate's stern.
21 (*left*). Fred F. French Building, 551 Fifth Avenue. 1927. Fred F. French Co. The decorative details of this building were borrowed from ancient Persia.

22 (*right*). Pan Am Building, 200 Park Avenue. 1963. Emery Roth & Sons, Pietro Bellischi, and Walter Gropius. A behemoth that contains 2,400,000 square feet of office space, or, to put it in other terms, 461.5 square miles.

23. 14 West 49th Street. 1937. Reinhard & Hofmeister; Corbett, Harrison & MacMurray; Hood & Fouilhoux. Bas-reliefs such as this are placed on buildings all over Rockefeller Center. According to the official guide to Rockefeller Center, this relief by Lee Lawrie (1937) symbolizes: "Each advanced civilization is made possible by the contribution of those imbued with inspiration, aspiration and divine fire."

24. Citicorp Building, 135 East 53rd Street. 1977. Hugh Stubbins & Associates. Scheduled for completion some time in late 1977, this skyscraper supplants Saint Peter's Lutheran church, whose new home is located at the northwest corner of the plot.

25. RCA Building, 30 Rockefeller Plaza. 1933. Reinhard & Hofmeister; Corbett, Harrison & MacMurray; Hood & Fouilhoux. Its smooth mass takes on a wondrous texture according to the light and time of day.

26. 1261 Madison Avenue. c. 1905. Truly the look of a "French flat"—so much so that it could take its place on L'Avenue d'Iena in Paris.

27. 15 East 90th Street. 1930. Mott B. Schmidt. The neo-Georgian look that became fashionable a generation after the Beaux-Arts explosion.

LOWER MANHATTAN

11 (above). View of Lower Manhattan toward the Battery. Sixty-five years ago Lower Manhattan presented an imposing skyline. This "new look" has appeared within the past decade.   12 (below). 20–36 Water Street. c. 1835. The surrounding area having been razed, one hopes this historic row will be spared from a similar fate.

13. American Express Building, American Express Plaza (125 Broad Street). 1972. Kahn & Jacobs. The building was partially completed in 1972, but did not receive an occupancy permit until 1976, when the present tenant moved in.

14. View from East River Drive near Broad Street. (left) American Express Building. 1972. Kahn & Jacobs. Manufacturers Trust Building. 1969. Carson, Lundy & Shaw. (center) Marine Midland Bank Building. 1967. Skidmore, Owings & Merrill. (right) 55 Water Street. 1972. Emery Roth. Towering over all in the background is the World Trade Center. 1975. Minoru Yamasaki & Associates, and Emery Roth & Sons.

15. 77 Water Street. 1969. Emery Roth & Sons. William Tarr, *Rejected Skin* (1969).

18. Lower Manhattan to Brooklyn Bridge. Almost 200 years of New York's architectural history—the World Trade Center at the left, the buildings on South Street in the center foreground, and the Brooklyn Bridge (1883) at the right—are encompassed in this view.

16 (left, above). 58 Pearl Street. c. 1827. Here is the "pristine look" that once characterized the whole city.   17 (left, below). India House, 1 Hanover Square (between Pearl and Stone streets). 1854. Richard J. Carman, carpenter. This is probably the apogee of the carpenter-builder tradition.

19. 96–110 Front Street. c. 1837. Unfortunately demolished in 1970, this remarkable row had the look of the innumerable blocks that were built following the great fire of 1835.

20 (above). 251 Water Street. c. 1840. Fortunately scheduled for preservation.
21 (below). 280 South Street. c. 1829. Alas, it did not last.

23. Marine Midland Bank Building, 140 Broadway. 1967. Skidmore, Owings & Merrill. The great cube is the work of Isamu Noguchi.

22 (left). Trinity Church, 74 Trinity Place. 1846. Richard Upjohn. Once one of the wealthiest landlords in New York, Trinity's surrounding cemetery contains the graves of Alexander Hamilton and Robert Fulton.

24. 1 Chase Manhattan Plaza Building, Liberty and Nassau streets. 1960. Skidmore, Owings & Merrill. The sculpture is by Jean Dubuffet, *Group of Four Trees* (1971).

25. Federal Reserve Building, 33 Liberty Street. 1924. York and Sawyer. It is appropriate that the building looks like the ultimate fortress, for it contains more gold than Fort Knox.

26. Woolworth Building, 233 Broadway. 1913. Cass Gilbert. A supreme example of the "busy bottom" school of early skyscraper architecture.

27 (right). Municipal Building, 23 Park Row. 1914. McKim, Mead and White. Early Wedding Cake, a style greatly admired by Stalin and his architects three decades later. The University of Moscow, however, pales by comparison.

30. 75–85 Worth Street. c. 1855. A beautiful adaptation of the Regency style.

28 (left, above). Criminal Courts Building and Prison (The Tombs), 100 Centre Street. 1939. Harvey Wiley Corbett. Prison Art Deco. 29 (left, below). Family Court, 60 Lafayette Street. 1976. Haines, Lundberg & Waehler. Not very familial, but a striking departure from the usual pedestrianism of government architecture.

31. Haughwout Building, 488–492 Broadway. 1857. J. P. Gaynor. This is probably the most famous and beautiful of the cast-iron facades still extant. The first Otis elevator was installed in this building, which was originally a department store.

MFRS. SUPPLY CO.

32. 670 Broadway. 1874. George E. Harney. When the neighborhood was fashionable, Brooks Brothers leased this space.

33 (right). 326 Spring Street. c. 1830. A pun is inevitable: The old place still has spirit.

34. Cable Building, 611 Broadway. 1894. McKim, Mead and White. The style may be described as "Columbian Exposition." It was the great Chicago extravaganza of 1893 that started the Classical Revival movement.

35 (right, above). Laing Building, 262 Washington Street. 1846. James Bogardus. Here is the little masterpiece—the first cast-iron front building—that was torn down in 1971, piled in a lot, then looted for its metal.

36 (right, below). 29–33 Harrison Street. 1797–1828. It is hard to realize that this handsome row was once a collection of condemned derelicts scheduled for destruction in the general razing of the Washington Market. They have been refurbished to their original gentility and are up for sale as residences.

38. State Insurance Fund Building, 199 Church Street. 1954. Lorimar Rich & Associates. Institutional inspirational.

37 (left). Cary Building, 105 Chambers Street. c. 1856. Gamaliel King and John Kellum. Not famous, not a landmark, but possibly the oldest iron front in the city.

39. 217 Church Street. c. 1870. A typical expanse of cast iron and glass.

40 (overleaf). Bayard Building, 65 Bleecker Street. 1898. Louis H. Sullivan. This great architect's only New York work. The building establishment was not ready for his advanced concepts.

41. Church of the Ascension, Fifth Avenue and 10th Street. 1840–1841. Richard Upjohn. Another landmark by the architect of Trinity Church.

42. 20 Fifth Avenue. c. 1938. The residents of lower Fifth Avenue heartily resisted the incursion of high-rise apartment houses, but this one is at least in good taste.

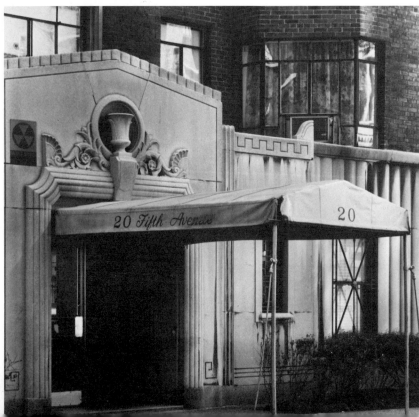

43. Congregation Senier & Wilno, 203 Henry Street. c. 1885. Lower East Side "synagogue-eclectic."

44. 97 East Broadway. c. 1890. Had this photograph been taken sixty years ago, there would have been little difference from what we see now.

45. Congregation Beth Harnesses, 290 Madison Street. 1856. Formerly the Olive Branch Baptist Church.

46. 45 Greene Street. 1882. J. M. Slade. Greene Street cast-iron Palladian.

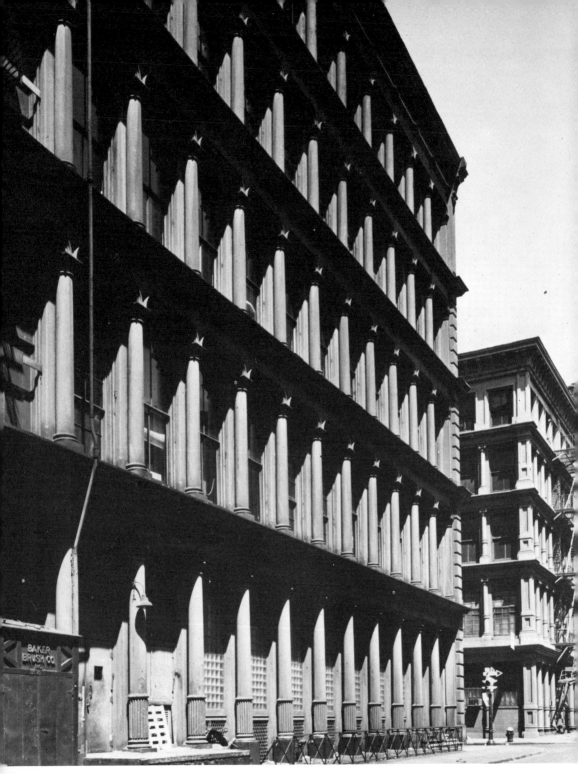

47. 87 Grand Street. 1872. William H. Hume. Classic iron-front lightness and grace.

48. 36 Greene Street. 1877. William H. Hume. An elegant iron-front addition to a rather plain loft.

49. 1 Bond Street. 1871. S. D. Hatch. This beautiful cast-iron front occupies the former site of the home of Albert Gallatin, Secretary of the Treasury and subsequently Minister to France under Thomas Jefferson.

50. 330 Bowery. 1874. Henry Engelbert. The former Bond Street Savings Bank now houses the Bouwerie Lane Theatre.

51. Detail of door, 137 East Houston Street. c. 1885. Regarded as a shoddy piece of mass production in its time, collectors avidly seize upon such a prize today whenever a building has been razed.

52. 11 East 11th Street. c. 1845. A very austere example of the Greek Revival style.

BROOKLYN HEIGHTS AREA

53. Brooklyn Bridge. 1883. John A. and Washington Roebling. Begun in 1860, this was the first steel-cable suspension bridge in the world, and it is still considered the most beautiful.

64

55. Eagle Warehouse & Storage Co., 28 Fulton Street. 1870. One hundred and seven years old, and still very much in business.

54 (left). Firehouse, Fulton Street Dock, Brooklyn. 1926. Hose-drying tower and all, this old-timer is now the Fulton Ferry Museum.

56. 62 Fulton Street. c. 1868. This front is not made of cast iron but pressed steel, a later technological development.

57. 48 Columbia Heights. 1865. Now standing alone among industrial buildings, it was once part of a neighborhood of similar houses.

58. 24 Middagh Street (former Boisselet House). 1824. Fancy Federal and considered by experts to be one of the finest examples extant.

59. 55 Middagh Street. c. 1840. The chopped-off appearance at the left indicates that it was once part of a row.

60. 104 Willow Street. c. 1829. Its adjoining neighbor indicates that this building resisted the brownstone onslaught.

61. 105 Willow Street. c. 1855. The elaborate doorway was probably an attempt around the 1890s at gussying up.

62. 109 Willow Street. 1905. Neo-Federal style, and sniffed at by local purists.

63. 120 Waverly Street. c. 1865. As was frequently the custom, the angelic faces may have been a likeness of the family's "little angel."

GREENWICH VILLAGE

64. 75½ Bedford Street. 1873. The smallest house in Greenwich Village and, for a time, the home of the poet Edna St. Vincent Millay.

65 (left). 115 Bedford Street and 126 Christopher Street. c. 1835. The Christopher Street house has been altered. 66 (below). St. John's in the Village, 224 Waverly Place. 1846. The original cost of construction was $15,000. It is currently up for sale.

67 (right, above). 17 Grove Street. 1822. The outstanding example of the few wooden houses remaining in the Village. 68 (right, below). 2–16 Grove Street. 1824–1836. One of the showplace streets in the Village.

69 (left). 65 Horatio Street. c. 1835. The top floor is surely a later addition. 70 (below). St. Luke's Chapel, 487 Hudson Street. 1822. James N. Wells. Clement C. Moore of "The Night Before Christmas" fame was its first vestryman.

71 (right, above). 25 Bank Street. c. 1850. The architecture suggests that this was the Village's answer to the brownstone. 72 (right, below). 6 Weehawken Street. 1810. No great shakes as architecture but of historical interest since its foundation may be pre-Revolutionary.

73 (left). Jefferson Market Library (formerly Jefferson Market Courthouse), 425 Avenue of the Americas. 1876. Vaux & Withers. The style is described in the authoritative *AIA Guide to New York City* as "Neuschwansteinian." No one will argue the point that It Is High Victorian. 74 (above). Jefferson Market Library, North End. 1876. Vaux & Withers. Voted the country's fifth most beautiful building in 1885, there are many today who, despite changing tastes, find its eclectic style very appealing.

75. MacDougal Alley, MacDougal Street between West 8th Street and Washington Square North. 1833. New York's answer to the mews of London.

76. St. John's Lutheran Church, 81 Christopher Street. c. 1821. A reminder that in its early days the Village embraced a fairly large colony of German immigrants.

MIDTOWN

77. Flatiron Building, 949 Broadway. 1902. D. H. Burnham & Co. An unusual view of the grand old lady, New York's first true skyscraper—her broad-beamed south end.

78 (above). 261 Fifth Avenue. 1928. A splashy entrance in Art Deco verticals and horizontals.   79 (below). Hugh O'Neill Building, 655 Avenue of the Americas. c. 1875. Mortimer C. Merrit. In its time a "far uptown" iron front.

80. Missions Building (Episcopal), 281 Park Avenue South. 1892–1894. R. W. Gibson, E. J. N. Stent. A well-designed pietistic approach to what was then an ecclesiastical high rise.

81. 207 East 17th Street. c. 1850. Restrained English Victorian.

82 (right). St. Mark's in the Bowery, Second Avenue and 10th Street. 1799. Ithiel Town. The grillwork is obviously nineteenth century.

83. 3 and 4 Gramercy Park West. 1846. Alexander Jackson Davis. Small wonder that, with a cast-iron establishment providing grill-work like this, New York exported tons of it to New Orleans.

84. The Players, 16 Gramercy Park South. 1845. The former Edwin Booth House is now a private club. Stanford White remodeled the house in 1888, and the extraordinary lantern must have been his addition.

85. 287 Lexington Avenue. c. 1895. A beautiful example of nineteenth-century cast-iron artistry.

86. Empire State Building, 350 Fifth Avenue. 1931. Shreve, Lamb & Harmon Associates. No longer the tallest, but still top banana.

87. 825 Third Avenue. 1969. Emery Roth & Sons. Demolition provides the rare opportunity to view a skyscraper in spacious perspective.

88. 7 West 46th Street. c. 1885. Once the residence of "Diamond Jim" Brady.

89 (right). RCA Building, 30 Rockefeller Plaza. 1933. Reinhard & Hofmeister; Corbett, Harrison & MacMurray; Hood & Fouilhoux. American Art Deco architecture at its breathtaking finest.

90. St. Patrick's Cathedral, 50th Street and Fifth Avenue. 1858–1879. James Renwick. Designed by a Protestant, but one who did his best to adapt the medieval Gothic tradition to city block requirements.

91. St. Regis-Sheraton, 2 East 55th Street. 1901–1904. Trowbridge & Livingston. This cab-calling booth reflects the rest of the hotel's elegance.

92 (right). Time & Life Building (left), 1271 Avenue of the Americas. 1960. Harrison, Abramovitz & Harris. (center) Equitable Building, 1285 Avenue of the Americas. 1961. Skidmore, Owings & Merrill. How they appeared before their gigantic neighbors arose to block the view.

93 (left to right). Celanese Building, 1211 Avenue of the Americas. 1973. McGraw-Hill Building, 1221 Avenue of the Americas. 1972. Exxon Building, 1251 Avenue of the Americas. 1972. Time & Life Building, 1271 Avenue of the Americas. 1960. Harrison, Abramovitz & Harris. Messrs. Harrison, Abramovitz & Harris's penchant for soaring, dizzying verticals may be the cause of what is called the "Sixth Avenue syndrome."

94 (above). Racquet Club, 370 Park Avenue. 1918. McKim, Mead and White. Florence on Park Avenue. 95 (below) St. Bartholomew's Church, 109 East 50th Street. 1919. Bertram G. Goodhue. The Byzantine-Eclectic entrance portico comes from an earlier church on Madison Avenue done by McKim, Mead and White in 1902. The dome and Chapter House were completed by Mayers, Murray & Phillip in 1927.

96. View: Park Avenue from the Seagram Building, 375 Park Avenue. The figure in the lower left-hand corner that seems to be pondering the mass of stainless steel and glass confronting it is an Easter Island statue. The incongruity may be explained by the fact that it was on loan from the Chilean government.

97. General Motors Building, 767 Fifth Avenue. 1968. Edward Durell Stone; Emery Roth & Sons Associated Architects. Apparently Mr. Stone opted in favor of the current vogue for massed verticals, eschewing the lacelike facades associated with his previous work.

98. Central Synagogue, 652 Lexington Avenue. 1872. Henry Fernbach. This door detail conveys the ornateness of the rest of the building.

99. 111 East 58th Street. 1968. William Lescaze & Associates. Resembling a part for some enormous machine, the sculpture is by Bernard Rosenthal.

100. 25–27 Beekman Place. Remodeled in 1927 by Pleasance
Pennington. Rehabilitation in the
grandest possible manner.

101. P. J. Clarke's, 915 Third Avenue. 1892. A pub designated a
landmark? You bet, especially
when it is just about the last of its
kind—the old-fashioned Third
Avenue saloon of hallowed memory.

102 (above, left). 1 Sutton Terrace. c. 1925. Quattrocento in Sutton Place. 103 (above, right). 29 Beekman Place. c. 1927. No row house monotony on Beekman Place! Here is the next-door neighbor to number 27.   104 (below). Riverview Terrace, 58th Street and East River. c. 1890. The rather bemused expression on this creature seems to contradict the warning posted on the gate he adorns: "Keep Out!"

UPPER EAST SIDE

105. 1057 First Avenue. This charming object is a good example of what makes random walking about the city such fun. You never know what visual delights may be encountered.

106 (above). Trinity Baptist Church, 250 East 61st Street. 1930. Martin Hedmark. Originally the First Swedish Baptist Church, its style may be described as Late Scandinavian Art Nouveau. The interior is stunningly beautiful.   107 (below). 1117 Second Avenue. c. 1905. The beginning of "singles-bars street."

108. Roosevelt Island Apartments. 1976. Master Plan: Philip Johnson, John Burgee. First it was Blackwell's Island, then Welfare Island, and now, with the creation of an amazing apartment-house complex, it is Roosevelt Island.

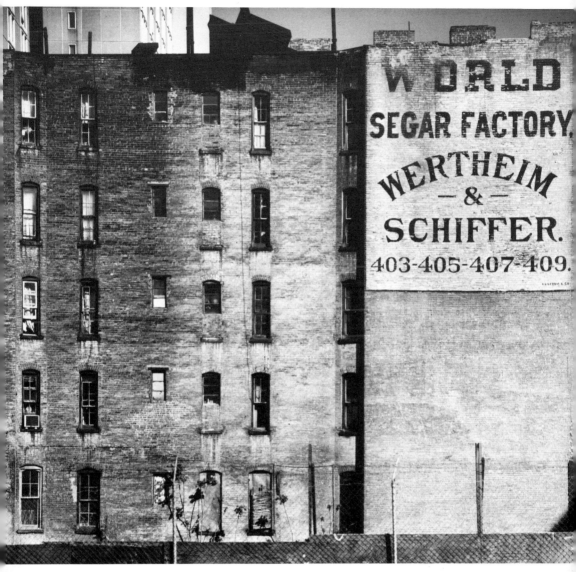

110. 403 East 70th Street. c. 1905. One of the first "model" tenements, which meant that it had hot and cold running water and adequate sanitary facilities.

109 (left). Octagon Tower, Roosevelt Island. 1839. Alexander Jackson Davis. Known with reason as "The Madhouse," it was the administration building for the city lunatic asylum. Visited by Charles Dickens, who pronounced it handsome, it was conceived in Tuscan style by Alexander Jackson Davis. The interior was modified in 1879 by Joseph M. Dunn in Classic Revival style. The staircase, dating from the period of remodeling, is magnificent. The building is now practically derelict.

111. 201 East 71st Street. c. 1900. The kind of "eye-catcher" that is the delight of architecture buffs.

112 (right). 130 East 64th Street. 1959. Edward Durell Stone. Here Mr. Stone presents a facade resembling that of his American Embassy in New Delhi, India.

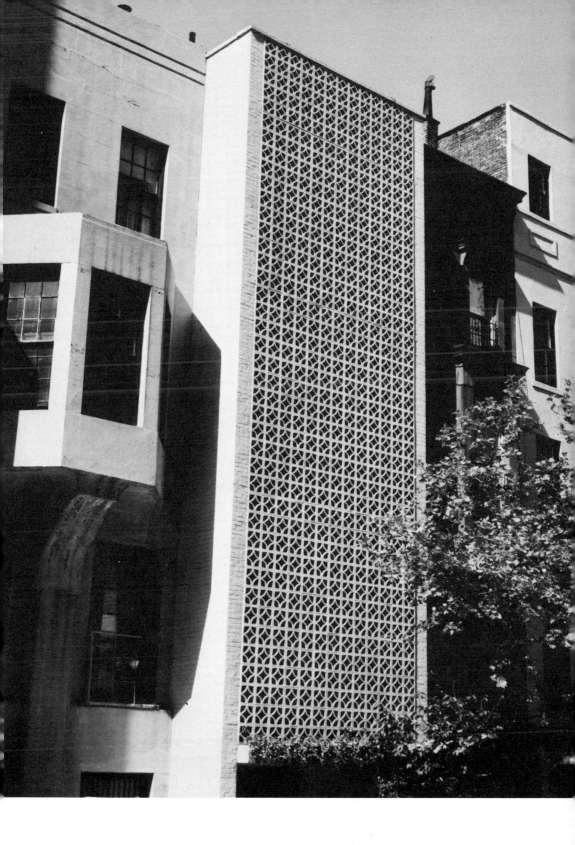

113. 729 Park Avenue. c. 1895. A very patrician cast-iron bay window.

114. 690 Park Avenue. 1917. Walker & Gillette. Now the Italian Consulate, it was formerly the Henry P. Davis House.

LYCÉE FRANÇAIS DE NE

115. Lycée Français de New York, 9 East 72nd Street. 1896. Carrère and Hastings. High Beaux-Arts and quite appropriate for the Lycée, it was originally the James Stillman House.

116. 6 East 77th Street. c. 1900. Now *there* is a console!

117 (left, above). Institute of Fine Arts, New York University, 1 East 78th Street, 1912. Horace Trumbauer. The former James B. Duke House was modeled after a chateaux in Bordeaux, a free approximation.   118 (left, below). Ukrainian Institute of America, 2 East 79th Street. 1879. C. P. H. Gilbert. Built for Augustus Van Horn Stuyvesant.   119 (above). 1009 Fifth Avenue. 1901. Welch, Smith & Provout. A bay window in the Beaux-Arts manner.

122. 22 East 89th Street. c. 1900. This product of the early 1900s is much more ornate than the usual East Side apartment house.

120 (left, above). 1130 Fifth Avenue. (1913). Delano & Aldrich. Neo-Federal according to Alan Burnham, neo-Georgian according to the AIA, originally the Willard Straight House; it is now the quarters of the International Society for Photography. 121 (left, below). J. Leon Lascoff and Son Pharmacy, 1209 Lexington Avenue. Facade: 1931 by Arthur Sutcliffe. Despite the intimation of medieval alchemy it is one of the most highly regarded establishments of its kind in the city.

123. 125 East 93rd Street. c. 1885. Fits Montgomery Schuyler's definition of Queen Anne (see page 12).

124. 115 East 75th Street. c. 1890. Now a garage, the horse's head on the keystone shows that the building was originally a stable.

125. 160 East 92nd Street. 1859. This house was obviously here when the area was fields and farmland.

126. Ruppert Brewery, 92nd Street and Third Avenue. c. 1895. This proud temple of the noble brew is, sad to say, no longer with us. It stood majestically atop the brewery, which was demolished to make way for an enormous apartment-house complex.

UPPER WEST SIDE

127. Bow Bridge, Central Park. 1859. Calvert Vaux. One of New York's greatest glories is Central Park, and Vaux's bridge is a major contribution to the surrounding beauty.

130. The American Museum of Natural History, Central Park West at 79th Street. 1877. J. C. Cady & Co. Romanesque Revival at its most robust and dignified.

128 (left, above). Ansonia Hotel, Broadway and 73rd Street. 1902. W. E. D. Stokes. The bacchanalian leer may have something to do with the goings-on of the famous "bohemians"—opera stars, concert performers, and artists—who once resided here. 129 (left, below). Hotel Lucerne, 201 West 79th Street. c. 1905. West Side Edwardian Baroque.

131 (left center). Majestic Apartments, 115 Central Park West. 1930. Office of Irwin S. Chanin. (right center) Dakota Apartments, 1 West 72nd Street. 1884. Henry Hardenburgh. The Art Deco Majestic, the Germanic-Renaissance Dakota—two trendsetters of their time.

132. Dakota Apartments, 1 West 72nd Street. 1884. Henry Hardenburgh. Detail of the cast-iron fence surrounding the Dakota.

133. 313 West 74th Street. c. 1905. A gracious example of the Continental look encountered in the Riverside Drive area.

134. (right). 341 West End Avenue. c. 1895. Once the home of Eberhard Faber, the lead-pencil tycoon.

135 (above). 110 West 81st Street. 1885. The Romanesque Revival style conveys a sense of enduring solidity as exemplified by the granite facade of this dignified town house. 136 (right). 40 Riverside Drive. c. 1890. Although Riverside Drive never had the cachet of Fifth Avenue, some of its mansions are equal to the best of Fifth Avenue's.

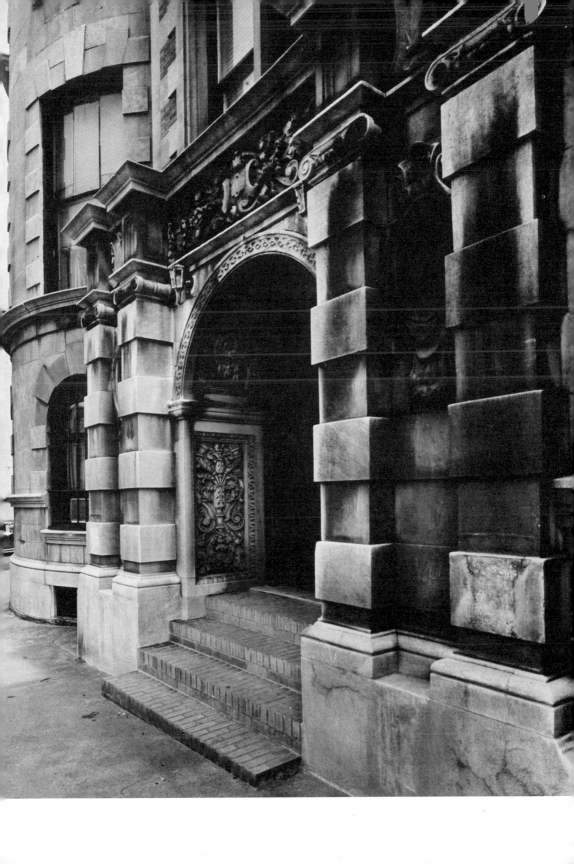

137. 46 Riverside Drive. c. 1895. A servants' entrance in elegant stonework.

138 (right). Columbia University, George Delacorte Gate, 116th Street and Broadway. 1916. Adams & Woodbridge. The crown atop the lamp symbolizes the fact that the university was originally the royally chartered King's Crown College, courtesy of George III.

140. Cuxa Courtyard, The Cloisters, Fort Tryon Park. A detail showing one of the
splendid capitals in the Cuxa Courtyard.

139 (left). The Cloisters, Fort Tryon Park. 1934–1938. Charles Collens. A mind-
boggling collation of monastery cloisters and a twelfth-century chapter house
magnificently transplanted from France. The photograph shows the courtyard of
the Romanesque Benedictine Abbey of St. Michel de Cuxa (A.D. 878).

DATE DUE